my darling, my daughter ...

Alessandra Hovey

AuthorHouse™
1663 Liberty Drive
Bloomington, IN 47403
www.authorhouse.com
Phone: 833-262-8899

This book is printed on acid-free paper.

ISBN: 978-1-6655-3871-8 (sc)
978-1-6655-3872-5 (e)

Library of Congress Control Number: 2021919351

Print information available on the last page.

Published by AuthorHouse 09/29/2021

authorHOUSE

my darling, my daughter ...

My darling, my daughter

I am here, I am near

You are never alone

Baby, you have nothing to fear

my darling,
my daughter ...

My darling, my daughter

I am here by your side

With me, my love,

You have nothing to hide

my darling,
my daughter ...

My darling, my daughter
This world can be dark
Just stay true to you and move forward
I have no doubt you'll leave a mark

my darling, my daughter ...

My darling, my daughter

You're my angel here on earth;

That's a fact but I am here to protect you

From the day you were born,

I vowed to do just that

my darling,
my daughter ...

My darling, my daughter

Please take my advice

I'll try not to be overbearing

But, remember,

I've done it once or twice

my darling, my daughter ...

My darling, my daughter

Remember, inner beauty counts the most

Be kind and be wise

And I'll try not to boast

my darling, my daughter...

My darling, my daughter

Learn to forgive and love yourself

And make sure to know your own worth

Self-love is important for your health

my darling,
my daughter ...

My darling, my daughter

Be sure to stand your ground

Sticking to what you believe in is hard, that I know

But well worth it I have found

my darling, my daughter ...

My darling, my daughter

You're a character and a half

I really enjoy your humor

Boy, do you make me laugh

my darling,
my daughter ...

My darling, my daughter

You became my best friend

It happened just like that

And I will hold that near and

dear till the very end

my darling, my daughter ...

My darling, my daughter

Don't change who you are

Not even a bit

Trust me, my beauty, you're a shining star

my darling,
my daughter ...

My darling, my daughter

You shine so bright

I'm so lucky you're mine

I love you, good night

Printed in the United States
by Baker & Taylor Publisher Services